Isn't That Interesting!

*Inspirational Teachings
From Above
by
Peg Perry*

*Research, Writing
Layout and Photography
By Bob Kranich*

Edited by Joanne Mary Kranich

Published by Bob and Joanne Mary Kranich
White Post, Virginia
bobkranich.com/books
bkranich.wixsite.com/bobkranich

Copyright 2017 by Peg Perry

All rights reserved. No part of this book may be reproduced in any form without permission in writing from the publisher.

Book design: Research, Writing
Layout and Photography
by Bob Kranich

Edited by: Joanne Mary Kranich

Published by:
Bob and Joanne Mary Kranich
White Post, Va.

Printed in the United States of America

Isn't That Interesting!
A story of the life of Peg Perry.
The building of Maria's Garden & Inn,
a Restaurant and Bed & Breakfast.
With inspirational teachings,
as given to: Peg Perry.

ISBN 978-0-9716515-3-1

First Paperback Edition

This book is dedicated to:
Mary, Mother of God

Table of Contents

Acknowledgements 9

Introduction 11

1. *Early Family 13*
2. *Childhood 15*
3. *Marriage 17*
4. *Building Maria's Garden 19*
5. *Religious Inspiration 25*
6. *The Teaching Gift 29*
7. *Teachings 30*

7.1 St Luke 30

7.2 St Luke, The First Icons 32

7.3 Teaching the Word of God 35

7.4 Verification of an Icon 36

7.5 Our Lady of Kazan 37

7.6 The Mind 40

7.7 Interpretation of the numbers 666 & 333 41

7.8 The Eagle Holds Up Our Lady 42

7.9 The Sun, The Moon, & The Son 43

7.10 On the Road to Emmaus 45

7.11 The Conversion of Russia..................................46

7.12 Our Lady of Guadalupe....................................47

7.13 Transfiguration...48

7.14 Keep Planting Seeds......................................49

7.15 The Vine Dresser...49

7.16 Radio, Jesus and Mother Mary.........................52

7.17 A Mother's Heart Is Warm Indeed.....................53

7.18 Special Water, Holy Ground............................55

7.19 Trinity Project, Mary's Protection......................56

7.20 Our Lady of La Salette Statue in Berkeley Springs..59

7.21 Saint Nicholas...61

7.22 Eucharistic Miracle at Lanciano........................63

7.23 Maria's Garden, Far and Wide.........................65

7.24 The Lady of the New Advent...........................66

7.25 U S A and the Immaculate Conception..............67

7.26 The Tear Drop Memorial.................................68

7.27 Our Lady, Queen of Peace, Statue...................69

7.28 Our Lady of the Milk......................................70

7.29 The song, "The Miracle of the Rosary"..............71

7.30 Edgar Allen Poe..72

7.31 One Day...74

7.32 Lazarus..74

7.33 Russian Conversion Continued............................75

7.34 Three Icons & St John Neumann..........................76

7.35 Mr. Fusek..77

7.36 The Shrine of the Immaculate Conception,
    The Czech chapel..78

7.37 St. Apollinaris an the Apollo Moon Mission.............79

7.38 The Body of Christ..80

7.39 The Bones Coming Together to be One.................82

7.40 George Washington and the New Advent..............84

8. Paintings, Statues, Pictures & Icons.......................86

9. A New Beginning..89

10. In Conclusion..91

Brochure, Maria's Garden.....................................92

 This file is in the **public domain** because its copyright has expired in the United States and those countries with a copyright term of no more than the life of the author plus **100** years.

Acknowledgements

In the writing of this book, *Isn't That Interesting*, I first would like to give credit to God, His mother Mary and the Holy Spirit for Their help and inspiration in my life.

I thank my husband, children, friends and patrons for encouraging me. I could not have persevered all these years without them.

God has allowed me to teach and hopefully these teachings have inspired my many listeners. I have been so privileged to help spread God's Word. I am overjoyed and overpowered to think that I may have been God's messenger to touch even just one person.

Thank you Jesus and Mary.

Peg Perry

Introduction

It is a such a great privilege and blessing to know Peg Perry. My mother Denise Sipe and I first met Peg in 1986 through a mutual friend. We have been visiting Maria's Garden ever since.

Peg loves Jesus and His Mother. Her life is dedicated with honoring Mary as she has felt she was instructed to years ago.

You will be touched by her sincerity, depth of spirit and Christ-like love. No matter what your spiritual beliefs are, you are welcome! She presents us with many teaching moments. This book records a few.

Joanne Mary Kranich

Grandmother, Laura
Grandfather, Efre Davalos Uncle Sam

Grandmother Father, Thomas Bastore   Mother, Constantina
   Peg   Sister, Lucy   Peg   Brother, Tom   Sister, Lucy

12   Isn't That Interesting!

1 Early Family

Peg's grandfather, Efre Davalos, was born in Buena's Aires, Argentina in 1884. Her grandmother, Laura was born in Hagerstown, Maryland in 1877. Efre emigrated to the USA and landed in the Port of Baltimore in 1903. He met and married Laura in Hagerstown. Efre died at an early age of 38 in 1916. He was overcome by gas while working at a cement plant.

After his death, grandmother Laura raised the two children, Sam and Peg's mother Constantina. She did remarry a man, John Musante who was instrumental in the invention of helicopter blades.

Peg's mom, Constantina met Thomas Bastore in Hagerstown, Maryland. They got married in 1929 and afterwards the family moved to Lititz, Pennsylvania. There Thomas worked at a shoe factory. They later moved back to Hagerstown where he worked at a dry cleaning company and later started his own dry cleaning company there in Hagerstown.

Lucy and Peg

2 Childhood

Peg was the second of four children. She was born in Hagerstown, Maryland in 1933. Lucy was the oldest, two years older than Peg. Tom was five years younger and the baby Cheryl was seven years younger than Peg. While Peg's Dad Thomas was busy with his own dry cleaning business, her mother was very involved raising the four children.

Peg went to Hagerstown High School and graduated in 1951. She was very interested in her studies and was a good straight "A" student. The last half of Peg's senior year she applied at a new finance company and got hired. Peg worked in the afternoons after school.

Peg   Lucy
   Tom   Cheryl

Peg & Jim, 1953

Alise 1960, 3 years

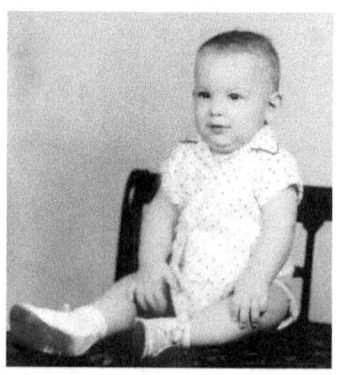

Curtis 1955, 9 months

3 Marriage

In 1951 Peg met Jim Perry. After Jim's graduation he went into the U.S. Marines. When he got out of basic training and advanced U.S. Marine training, he came home on leave and proposed to Peg.

In March 14, 1953, Peg married James Edward William Perry. They were married in St. Mary's Catholic Church in Hagerstown, Maryland. Jim was in the U. S. Marine Corps and Peg then moved with Jim to Jacksonville, North Carolina to Camp Lejeune, Marine Corps base. He spent the first part of the marriage fighting for his country in Korea. After Jim was discharged they returned to Hagerstown, Maryland.

In February 1955 James Curtis was born, and in November 1957 Alesa Margaret was born.

In the mid-sixties Peg took a one year course in a beauty school in Martinsburg. She then operated her own hair salon in Berkeley Springs, West Virginia.

In the early part of their marriage Jim worked as a barber. When he got tired of doing that he asked Peg if she would like to open a pizza/sub take-out shop. She thought that would be a good idea and they rented a place in Berkeley Springs on main street.

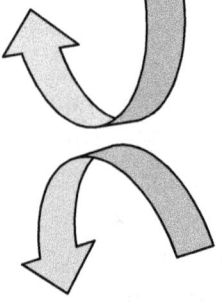

4 Building Maria's Garden

In November of 1982, after their trip to Fatima, Portugal, strange circumstances resulted in Jim and Peg purchasing a 1929 two-story brick home. It had a large auto repair garage on the lower level.

Curtis said, "Mom, why don't we buy that house on the corner and move the pizza shop there?"

The catalyst for the purchase was the idea of moving Perry's Pizza Parlor to that location. Peg also wanted to expand the menu to offer the Eastern Panhandle good spaghetti.

The garage was converted into what is now two dining rooms while the basement became the kitchen. The original intent was modest, but the Perrys couldn't resist continuing to add on.

During the winter of 1984-85, they remodeled the upstairs of the brick house. As they finished up the remodeling, they purchased the adjacent twin brick house. This kept them real busy. They now had a good size B & B. They fixed up and named the four rooms on the second floor of the adjacent house after their daughter Alesa's four children: Laura, Aaron, Stephen, and Louisa. All of the other rooms have special names.

They decorated the rooms as you would an elegant B & B with beautiful antique beds, spreads, furniture, accessories and bathrooms with claw foot tubs.

While transforming the quaint patio between the two houses into a garden dining room, Peg found a niche in the stone wall running along the street. She placed a statue of Our Lady of Fatima in the niche with three children kneeling at her feet.

The next day Peg went out to the court yard and saw a rose growing from under the statue with a single bloom. (In the story of the Lady of Fatima, roses play a significant part.

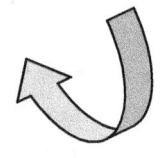
Before

Today

Before

Today

See Chapter 5, Religious Inspiration) This rose inspired Peg to create a garden in the courtyard and reorganize the restaurant plans to make the statue of Mary more visible to patrons. The name was changed and Maria's Garden (formerly Perry's Family Restaurant) opened in December 18, 1986. This is the Feast of the Lady of the New Advent.

Today one may dine in the garden. There are glass top tables set about the outdoor garden, which is just on the outside of the main dining. One may enter from the main dining room through sliding glass doors.

In 1998 a second story was built on top of the first restaurant area. Three new rooms were added and named Michael, Raphael and Gabriel after the archangels. These new rooms offer cathedral ceilings, queen size beds, cable TV, whirlpool tubs, working stone fireplaces and one Jacuzzi.

In 2001, Peg built a Chapel in the upper area of the Garden dining room for people to visit, pray and

The Shrine to Our Lady Of Guadalupe which is just inside the first dining room on the right. This is the image of the Blessed Virgin Mary that appeared on Juan Diego's tilma (cloak)

have private Masses. There is room to have a small wedding; it seats about 24 people.

Maria's Garden & Inn is the product of faith and hard work. It is not just the faith of the Perry's that has built Maria's, but of the many guests and friends. They bring all kinds of gifts to add to the collection of pictures, keepsakes, relics, icons, statues, rosaries, medals, holy water, paintings and many other religious articles.

Peg's family has always had this unique motto:
"*Work as though everything depends on you;*
Pray as though everything depends on God."

From her place in a stone grotto next to a fountain. A life-size statue of Mary, the Mother of God, greets visitors.

5 Religious Inspiration

As you walk through the front door of Maria's Garden in Berkley Springs, each visitor steps not only into a restaurant, but into a religious experience. A life-size statue of Mary, the Mother of God, greets visitors from her place in a stone grotto next to a fountain.

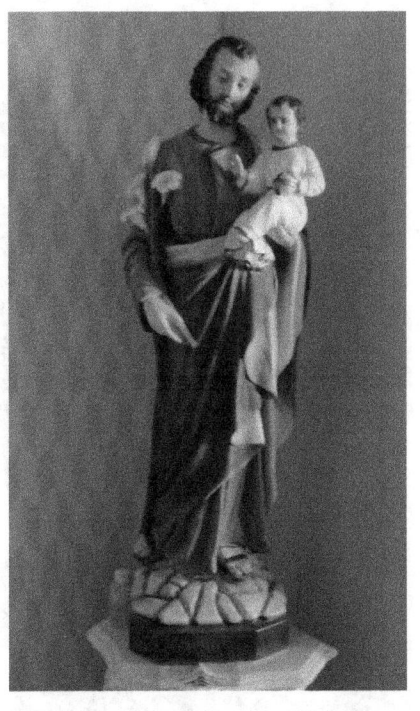

Prepare to see an infinite number of pictures, statues, icons and artifacts given to Peg by friends and guests of all faiths from all over the United States and the world! However there is no feeling of intrusive religiosity. It is just a spiritual inspiring experience.

During late 1981 to early 1982 Peg experienced severe health problems. It was at this time in her life that she spent much time at home reading and praying.

The Garden is the result of a trip in 1982 where Peg, Jim and a local priest had the privilege of visiting Fatima, Portugal. This is where the Blessed Virgin Mary appeared in 1917 to three children. There Peg received the inspiration to both change her life and build a place of spiritual renewal.

The Maria's Garden is a small beautiful enclosure just outside the restaurant's main dining room's sliding glass doors. In it is a grotto with a statue of Our Lady of Fatima

and statues of the three Portuguese children to whom she appeared in the early 1900's.

As you enter the restaurant's first dining room, to the right is a shrine to Our Lady Of Guadalupe tucked into the wall. This recalls a story of divine intervention that Peg holds dear.

According to tradition, the Blessed Mother appeared to Juan Diego, a poor Aztec Indian in 1531. She told him to entreat the Bishop at Mexico City to build a church on the spot at which she stood. The Bishop did not believe Juan's story, so as a sign to the disbelieving Bishop, the Lady told Juan Diego to climb to the top of a barren hill (it was midwinter), and pick the flowers which he would find growing there. At the top of the hill Juan discovered beautiful Castilian Roses growing in the snow. He picked them and Mother Mary arranged them herself in his tilma (cloak).

Later in the presence of the Bishop and others, Juan Diego opened his tilma to present the roses. The flowers fell to the floor. As Juan bent to retrieve them, he noticed the Bishop on his knees in adoration. On his tilma was the image of the Blessed Virgin Mary. Shortly afterward the Bishop ordered the church to be built. Not only has scientific analysis of various studies failed to indicate a man-made origin, the image led to the conversion of over nine million Aztec Indians to the Roman Catholic Faith.

In 2001 Peg had a Chapel built in the upper area of the Garden dining room over-looking Maria's Garden Grotto for people to visit and pray. When you enter in you have the same pious feeling one has when they enter any religious sanctuary.

Peg has said, "I couldn't have done this all on my own, it became God's project. I didn't plan it and didn't design it, I think it's all been pre-designed!"

Peg engaged in a "Teaching Moment" in the main dining room of Maria's Garden.

Peg has a treasure of reference material relating to her "Teachings" in her office files and she won't hesitate to make use of them.

6　The Teaching Gift

As you are dining at Maria's Garden Inn and Bed & Breakfast, you may have the privilege to speaking to a petite very nice looking lady with a beautiful hairdo. Sometimes she is fresh out of the kitchen wearing her apron or food preparing t-shirt.

If you are so blessed she may give you one of her "teachings". Peg Perry is constantly being inspired with a new teaching from above which she can relate to the Holy Bible.

Peg says that this gift began in 1977...I was listening to the radio in my car and I heard a voice say: "Turn the radio off and be still." I did as it said.

Then the voice said, "My child, tell My people to love My Mother." Then it repeated it, "Tell my people to love My Mother."

I said, "Lord how will I do that?"

The voice replied, "I will go before you...I will engineer the circumstances. My child, you tell them that God is Love. When they love My Mother, it's God's love."

Peg then replied, "Lord Jesus, would You teach me to love Her as you love Her, know Her as you know Her. Teach me to be more like your Mother." (The Virgin Mary)

Peg believes the teaching gift as been handed down from the blood line on her mother's side because St. Theresa Avila was the patron saint of mystic teaching. Her mother's maiden name was Davalos and comes from de Avila, Spain. Her father's side was from Avila, Spain. People's last name many times came from the city they were born in.

Peg said, "I meet all kinds of people. All I'm called to do is love them where they are and plant the seeds. This is *Maria's Garden*. I don't pull the weeds. I don't try to change them."

7 Teachings

The following "teachings" have been recorded by Peg as she taught them to people at Maria's Garden.

We pray that they inspire and educate you as they have us.

7.1   St. Luke

Across the street from Hunter's Hardware here in Berkeley Springs, is a small white building. It used to be an antique shop called Young Bloods Antiques.

One day I went in to look around. I saw a special case with all these little books. I asked the lady "What are these little books?" She said that it was a doctor's library. A book I saw kind of lit up spiritually to me. It was titled, "The Dear and Glorious Physician" by Taylor Caldwell.

During that time I was learning about the first icons, and that they were made by St. Luke. (the Madonna Icons) St .Luke was a doctor, a scholar and at first he was not a Christian. He didn't know Jesus. By the time he found out about Jesus, Jesus was gone and risen up into heaven.

He walked with St. Paul. He found out that Jesus' mother, Mary was still living and he went in search for her. He found her in Ephesus. When he first saw her, she said, "You have come to write the account." He stayed there in Ephesus and Mary taught him so he could write his gospel. St. Luke is the only Gospel that has Mary's words in it!

Luke is known to have been writing to a man named Theopolis, "Oh Theopolis, I thought it would do well to set down the account that what has been handed down to you by the eye witnesses is true."

That letter becomes the Gospel of St. Luke.

The Black Madonna of Poland, "Our Lady of Czestochowa" According to legends, it was created by Luke the Evangelist, the first iconographer between 66 and 67 AD. It gets its name because of the sooty residue of smoke from candles and incense over the centuries.

For Copyright information and United States public domain tag See page 8

7.2   St. Luke, The First Icons

During the time I was learning about the first icons being made by St. Luke I didn't plan to put all the icons we have here at Maria's Garden on the walls.

One day a man came in with a 4" x 6" icon painted on straw. It was an icon of the Black Madonna of Poland, "Our Lady of Czestochowa". He brought it to me as a gift. I could not hang it because of the straw, so I put it in a lighted glass case. He also gave me a pin of the "Lady of Fatima".

Another day a nun came in with a priest and asked "Where is 'Our Lady of Czestochowa." She was very excited to see it and they spoke some time about in a different language, Polish I guessed.

So some time later a man came in with a bus tour and had a package for me. It was an icon of "Our Lady of Czestochowa." This is identified by the three black marks on her face made by slashes of a sword in sieges in the 13 & 1400's in the town of Czestochowa, Poland.

This man told me that it was originally painted by St .Luke at Mary's house in Ephesus. St. Luke used the table (made by Jesus when he was a carpenter) at Mary's house to paint on while she taught him about Jesus' life.

When St. Helena went to Jerusalem in 326 she found the icon and sent it to her son, Constantine in Constantinople. He had a shrine built to house it.

Then begins an interesting history of the portrait:

* In a critical battle with the Saracens the portrait was displayed on the walls of Constantinople and the Saracens were routed.

* The painting went to the royal palace in Ruthenia (northwest Hungary). In the eleventh century when an invasion occurred, the king prayed to Our Lady to aid his

A painting of St. Luke painting the first icon of Our Lady and the Baby Jesus. We see an angel guiding him. 16th century Russian painting, author anonymous.

For Copyright information and United States public domain tag See page 8

One of Luke's paintings of Mary is of the type as this one, known as, "Our Lady of Tenderness". None of the originals exist. This Is a Russian icon and is the famous "Our Lady of Vladimir". Note that even though, Mary does not have Russian features. Therefore, it is supposed that the features date back to the original likeness painted by St Luke

For Copyright information and United States public domain tag See page 8

Isn't That Interesting!

* In the fourteenth century it was transferred to Poland to the Prince of Ladislaus of Opola. In 1382 the Tartars invaded and attacked the Prince's fortress at Belz. In this attack an arrow hit and stuck into the throat area of the painting. The prince fearing that the famous painting might fall into the hands of the Tartars, fled to the town of Czestochowa. There the Prince later had a Pauline monastery built to ensure the paintings safety.

  * In 1430 the Hussites overran the monastery and attempted to take the portrait. One of the looters struck the portrait twice with his sword, but then fell to the floor and died.

  * In 1655, Poland was overrun by the forces of Sweden. Somehow, the monks of the monastery were successful in defending the portrait against a 40 day siege until the siege was lifted.

  * After these remarkable turn of events, the Lady of Chestochowa became the symbol of Poland.

  * In 1920 the Russians were threatening Poland and an image of the Virgin was seen in the clouds over the city and the Russian army withdrew.

  * In 1980 Lech Walesa, the leader of the Solidarity Movement who wanted to get their freedom from the Communists and Russia wore a lapel pin of Our Lady of Czestochowa.

  * In 1970, 1983, and again in 1991 the Pope visited Our Lady of Czestochowa.

  *There are many reports of spontaneous healings by visitors to the Black Madonna.

If you wonder why she is called the "Black Madonna". The name comes from the smoke and soot of centuries of votive lights and candles burning in front of the painting.

Her Icon is in the second dining room as you look into Maria's Garden.

7.3 Teaching the Word of God

God told me one day, that the Word of God is just like salt. If salt is taken internally one becomes more thirsty. If it is applied externally to an open wound there is a painful reaction.

If you meet people and are sharing things about God and you see that they have a negative reaction, it is because they have an open wound. You never share and put salt on an open wound! You need to back off and put balm in the wound. The balm you should use is *Love*.

In the Bible the Sadducees asked Jesus, "Which is the greatest commandment". Jesus said, "You should love the Lord your God with all your heart, with all you soul and with all your mind. The second most important is you should love your neighbor as yourself. The whole of the law and prophets depends on these two commandments."

One time someone came to me and said this, "I have done a lot of wrong things in my life." We know that Love covers a multitude of sin. It begins by baptism, which covers all our original sin by the blood of the Lamb; but what about sins we make after baptism?

We have a commandment from God to Love others as he loved us. In the 70's I went to visit a lot of the different churches of my non-Catholic friends. (I did not leave my church, I just visited, I still attended Mass). You know, that by baptism we "All" are members of the Body of Christ.

The first church I visited was Pentecostal. It was really different! But God told me, that I must love "All" these people, I want you to know these people.

I got down on my knees and prayed to Jesus, "I don't want to do anything wrong, but would you show me the truth." He said that, "I am the truth, the light and the way." That is when I started learning mystically from God. I started to learn about my Catholic faith, how it originated and the beauty of it.

Now, I tell everyone when they have a problem to ask Jesus for the truth. God is truth, He will not deny Himself. God will begin to show you the truth.

7.4 Verification of an Icon

There is an icon of Mary whose features look somewhat far eastern. It is on the wall on the right as you look out to Maria's Garden. I was told that it was painted by someone when they visited the holy house at Ephessis. At first I wasn't sure of its authenticity. I always wanted to be responsible for what I put up at Maria's Garden that it was both accurate and authentic.

I wanted to thank Sister Mary Ann for giving me a copy of the Black Madonna. I heard that she was at the Shrine of the Immaculate Conception. I went there looking for her. While there I found out that she was the Mother Superior.

As I was looking for her I wandered into a small little room. It was a tiny office. Lo-and-behold, on the wall in that little office room was a copy of the exact picture that I was worried about!

I said to myself, "If that picture is good enough for the shrine of the Immaculate Conception, It is good enough for Maria's Garden!"

So that is how that icon went up on the wall at Maria's Garden. I wanted to tell you that, because there is a story behind everything on the walls of Maria's Garden. I love for people to come in and just look the items on the walls. If you ever come in to Maria's Garden and have a question, call me aside. I'll be glad to tell you about them.

A copy of the Icon of Our Lady of Kazan (16th century)

For Copyright information and United States public domain tag See page 8

7.5 Our Lady of Kazan

In 1381 St. Sergius founded the Holy Trinity Monastery in Sergiyev Posad, Russia. One hundred and fifty years later in 1431 the Blessed Mother appeared to a little blind girl and asked her to dig in these old ruins in the town of Kazan.

Under the old ruins they found this icon of the Madonna and child absolutely intact. The little blind girl miraculously had her sight restored.

During this time the land was being invaded. Saint Surge appeared to the Holy Bishop, and said if they carried that icon before their army they would have a great victory. They did and since the victory was attributed to the icon, they named her the "Leboratress and Protectoress of Russia".

A church was built to house the icon in Moscow. All through history when they had a favor granted from Our Lady's intercession they added jewels to the outlines of the icon (rubies, diamonds emeralds). They added these from the time of Katherine the Great through Peter the Great.

When Peter the Great came to the throne, he founded St. Petersburg and he named it his capital. He built a cathedral under the title of Our Lady of Kazan. He had the icon brought to St. Petersburg. Later a copy was made, left in St. Petersburg and the original was taken back to Moscow.

In 1917 the Communists called out to the people in Red Square that there is no God. In 1929 they closed the cathedral and changed the name of St. Petersburg to Leningrad. After that no one knew what had happened to the icon. It had disappeared.

In 1950 a Russian countess saw an icon in England on a castle wall. She believed it was the original. The Blue Army of the Lady of Fatima contracted to keep the icon safeguarded in Portugal until Russia would get their country back some day.

In 1977-1982 the icon was brought to San Francisco and kept in a vault.

In 1982 I found out that the Russian icon was going to be in Washington, New Jersey at the National Shrine of Our Lady of Fatima. We went there on May 1st and saw the icon. We then went to Fatima and the Byzantine Chapel. On May 13 we stayed in the Blue Army of Our Lady of Fatima headquarters. The icon was brought down to our chapel as we prayed all night for the conversion of Russia. Then the Fatima tune that chimes from the Basilica every 15 minutes was being sung by a priest from Chicago to the icon. The Holy Father led a million and a half people that night. They sang the verses in Portuguese but I was hearing the words in English. When I looked over he had my poem in his prayer book. We stayed there all night and at four o'clock in the morning I had the privilege of carrying the icon up to the Byzantine Chapel.

In 1993 the icon was given to Pope John Paul the Second. He venerated it for 11 years in his studio.

In August 2004 it was returned to Russia. It is enshrined in the Church of the Elevation of the Holy Cross, which is part of the Monastery of the Theotokos on the site where the original icon of Our Lady was found.

How did the icon get from Russia to England? My Aunt Olga's father was the attaché to the Czar of Russia. During the coronation of George the Fifth in 1910, he rode in the royal car and the Czar rode in a common car for safety. In fact the two leaders, Czar Nicholas II and King George V were cousins. Therefore I believe the royal family smuggled the icon out before the Communists could get it.

Of a special note: The Russians are now in the ISS (International Space Station). The Russian Cosmonauts took an icon of our Lady of Kazan up on the space shuttle to the space station. She is now there in the International Space Station. There were six people who flew to the space station, three Russians, two Americans and one Japanese. One of the American astronauts had just become a convert to the Catholic Church. He didn't want to leave Jesus in the real presence of the Holy Eucharist all those months. He got permission to take a container with six consecrated hosts with him. This way he could break each one into four parts to last all the time he was in space.

Isn't That Interesting!

I found this very interesting because not only is Our Lady in the space station but her Son (the real Presence) in the Holy Eucharist is there too.

7.6 The Mind

The Lord has told us that, We should love the Lord our God, with all our whole heart,
  with all our whole soul,
  with all our whole mind.
I wonder how many pick up on the word mind? I woke up one morning and this is what I said to God:

> Lord, something is happening to my mind,
> There are thoughts that I can't find.
> A game of cat and mouse, you see,
> That I'm the one who is up the tree.
>
> I search and search sometimes for days,
> The answers only cause amaze.
> This mind is playing tricks, you see,
> A peek-a-boo, can you see me.
>
> You almost have it and then it's gone,
> Thank God my guardian angel prayer
> Gives peace of mind, I know he is there.
>
> My mind is my computer disk,
> And so my future mind's at risk.
> The eyes that scan the TV screen,
> saw pictures they should not have seen.

"Put on the mind of Christ," Paul said,
But many scriptures I've not read.
My mind was not as yet filled up,
With words from God's sweet loving cup.

But time has not run out as yet,
To pray for thoughts, I must forget.
And plant the Garden from above,
With seeds of faith, and hope, and love.

Lord in you alone I came to be,
I'll place my heart, and mind in thee.
Peg Perry

7.7 Interpretation of the numbers 666 & 333

In the book of Revelations you have all of these different Christians' interpretation of the Bible. Their interpretations are according to the level in which they see. Let's take it to another level, that which our Lady sees, and what she explains.

In the Marian Movement of Priests, which were messages given to Father Stefano Gobb, Our Lady gives the mystery of the 666. She said that God's number was three, 333.
This is the number of the Trinity, The Father, Son and Holy Ghost. Satan wanted to be higher so he took the number 666.

Our Lady explains that the rise of Satan took place in 666, 1332 and 1998. I realized these were periods of time.

I have this book by Readers Digest, I think the name of it is "The World's Last Mysteries". The last chapter is about Emperor Constantine. The question I asked was, when did Constantine become Emperor? Up to his reign the

Christians were being persecuted.

Now his mother, who is now called St. Helena became a Christian. She found the spot where Jesus was born and also the spot where Jesus was buried. Over these spots she built the Church of the Nativity and the Church of the Holy Scepter.

Constantine was in a battle in 328, when up in the sky he saw a glowing cross. There was also a sign, "By these words ye shall conquer". Because of this he became a great Christian. He allowed Christianity to come forth. He built St. Peter's Basilica and St. John's church. He united the East and the West during the years 328–338.

During the year 333, this was the triumph of the church and 333 is God's perfect number.

7.8 The Eagle Holds Up Our Lady

There is something I misunderstood about the image in our stone wall of Our Lady of Guadalupe. All these years I thought that what was holding her up beneath her cloak was an angel.

One day I was teaching some people about the symbols in the dollar bill. I was telling them that "In God We Trust" wasn't always on the dollar bill. In fact it was made a law in 1955 and was put on the bill in 1957. Most people don't know that.

I was telling them that the eagle holds the olive branch. I suddenly had the urge to go and take a look at the picture of Our Lady of Guadalupe. (see page 22)

Guess what I saw on the image and realized. There are red, white and blue wings on the bottom of the picture. These are eagle wings beneath Our Lady.

In Revelation in the Bible, each Gospel, Matthew, Mark,

Luke and John has a symbol. The symbol for John is the eagle in flight. That is John's Gospel.

The symbol of the eagle appears in our Bible and in the symbolism of our country, the United Sates of America.

7.9 The Sun, The Moon, & The Son

Many years ago, down in Florida, I was awaken and given these words.
That the sun rises on everyone, good or bad.
When the sun is up, we see
When the sun is down, we don't see.
What is the moon?
The moon is a reflection of the sun.
When the sun is down, what lights the sky?
It is the moon.
I always see that Our Lady is like the moon, She reflects her Son. You can't look at the sun without an aid. So you have to look at Our Lady so you can see the Son.

I was impressed by all of this revelation, here is my poem.

Dear Father Sun

Dear Father Sun and Mother Moon
    And all our brother stars
There is so much to learn of You
    From Jupiter to Mars

I woke this morn to gaze about
    As dawn was peeping through
The end of night, the start of day
    Another gift from You

There is so much to learn of You
      Our feeble mind is weak
Like babies under mother's arms
      To guard us as we seek

The earth, the sun, the moon and stars
      Are made to know you, Lord
We come from dust and back to dust
      So sin, we can't afford

In life, our struggles, sometimes great
      We think we cannot stand
As life goes on and we look back
      We see your helping hand

Without the sun to guide each day
      Each life would all be night
Not knowing those around us
      In dark there is no sight

Inside each man there is a life
      A breath that never dies
Made by a God who loves us
      Creator of the skies

Our breath of life is like the day
      We have a Son to guide
To give us light and guard each day
      From Him, we never hide

In God our Father who is Son
      We reflect like moon
And as sons like brother stars
      We live in one big room

7.10 On the Road to Emmaus

From Luke's Gospel:
Two men are on their way to Emmaus. One's name is Cleophas.

As I read this, in my head I'm hearing :
At the foot of the cross was Jesus's mother, Mary, her sister Mary, wife of Cleophas and Mary Magdalene (John's Gospel). I wonder, is that the same Cleophas on the away to Emmaus, the husband of the Blessed Mother's sister?

Jesus comes upon the scene on the way to Emmaus and asks the two men, "What are you talking about?"

They say, "Haven't you heard? Are you the only one who hasn't heard about Jesus of Nazareth being condemned by the chief priests and rulers to be crucified?"

He continued to ask them questions. When they got to the village they asked Him to stay over with them because it was toward evening. When He broke the bread and gave thanks they recognized Him. Then He disappeared.

They said, "Did not our hearts burn when He broke the bread and blessed it?"

Then what did they do, they hurried back to Jerusalem to the upper room to tell the apostles. "We have seen the Lord!"

I wonder, just how did they get into the upper room when the door was locked.
One of the disciples was James the son of Alphaeus. Alphaeus is another name for Cleophas.

I believe that Cleophas was the father of one of the apostles, James.

7.11 The Conversion of Russia

In 1917 Lenin set up the Communist revolution. At Fatima, when Our Lady prayed for a conversion of Russia, she appeared during the Miracle of the Sun. She appeared as the Lady of Mount Carmel. She also appeared with St. Joseph and the baby Jesus. In 1986 the disaster of Chernobyl weakened the Soviet Union so that they never could recover.

A friend brought me a newspaper clipping about the Chernobyl accident. A Ukrainian friend of mine also told me that Chernobyl means Wormwood. Then I remembered in Revelation Chapter 8, a star fell out of the sky, its name was Wormwood and it polluted the waters. She said, "Yes Peg, names have meanings." For example, Gorbachev means hunchback. In my head I'm thinking Hunchback of Notre Dame. It's kind of a bad nickname to put on someone. But then he was a good preacher.

Padre Pio said, "When there's a blue army member for every communist, Russia will be converted. I thought, Communism began by the meeting of red cells. So I'm in church and I ask a friend to pray the rosary with me. When two people pray the rosary together that is a blue army cell. When one color cells in the human body outnumber others, they kill the lesser cells. Then I knew when there are enough blue army cells, the red cells will dissipate.

Gorbachev came from a very religious background. He was laid at the foot of Mary and consecrated by his mother. In 1991 when Gorbachev was put under house arrest, that is when the Berlin Wall came down. Gorbachev was the "Hunchback" of Notre Dame.

7.12 Our Lady Of Guadalupe

In 1531, down in Mexico, Our Lady appeared to an uneducated Indian, Juan Diego. At that time the Indians were offering human sacrifices to their gods. I had the privilege of climbing the Pyramid of the Sun.

I will tell you what changed the Indians offering up human sacrifices to their god. What made this change is when Our Lady appeared to Juan Diego. She wanted a church build on this spot. She did not condemn the Indians for offering human sacrifices because they only knew their sun god. No one had ever told them about a loving God.

She said, "I am your merciful Mother."

She asked Juan Diego to go to the Bishop and tell him that she wanted to have a church built on this spot. When he went and told the Bishop Our Lady's request, the Bishop didn't believe him.

She appeared to Juan Diego again and said that he should climb to the top of a hill in mid-winter and pick the roses that would be there. He climbed to the top of the hill in the snow and picked beautiful Castilian roses which only come from Spain.

When he brought them to her she rearranged them inside his cloak and told him not to let anyone see the roses until he saw the Bishop. When he got to the Bishop, the roses fell out onto the floor. The Bishop fell to his knees because the image of *Our Lady of Guadalupe* was imprinted on the inside of the cloak.

(see page 22)

The Church was built.

The image converted 9,000,000 Indians to Christianity in seven years. They gave up their human sacrificing. Our Lady was bringing her Son to the new world.

7.13 Transfiguration

The Feast of the Transfiguration is August 6th. The Scripture says, Jesus took Peter and John up on the mountain and there He was transfigured before them. There they saw Moses and Elijah talking to our Lord. It said His Face shone like the sun. He was so bright that they couldn't look at Him. Then a dark cloud came over Him and a voice from Heaven said, "This is My Beloved Son, listen to Him." They looked up and they saw Jesus.

As this was being read during Mass, I came upon something I had never thought of before. The meaning of the word transfiguration. You know what it means? His figure was changed. That was our Lord, but His figure changed from the way He looked as a man to the sun. They couldn't look at the sun.

That is similar when Jesus was baptized in the Jordan River by John the Baptist and a voice from Heaven said, "This is My Beloved Son."

What I wanted to think about, is this word transfiguration. Then I thought, "Now I get it!" In Mass when the bread and wine is changed it is call, transubstantiation. It still looks like bread and wine but the substance is changed. It is now our Lord's heart, body and blood.

I had never picked up on that and I went, "Oh that is interesting!"

7.14 Keep Planting Seeds

I heard God speaking, "Any word that edifies is a seed. If it does not edify, it is a weed. We should sort out the weeds from the seeds. Allow only seeds to feed into your mind."

I said, oh my goodness God! I've planted a lot of weeds in my time, but I didn't know that I was planting weeds. So I have to be careful. If I'm not speaking words of Faith, Hope and Love, I've planted a weed.

Who plants the weeds? The enemy. From the Bible: One day the owner comes to the vineyard and sees that his workers planted seeds. But in the night the enemy came and planted weeds. What should we do? Pull out the weeds? No. Let them alone, because you may accidently pull out the good plants. Leave them alone until harvest. In the end the good plants will be harvested and the weeds will be thrown into the fire.

So we have to watch that we don't pull out the good plants with the weeds. Just keep planting seeds, because what I have found is if you planted seeds the flowers will take over.

7.15 The Vine Dresser

Early in my marriage life, both my marriage and my husband weren't what I had expected. After I went through what I am going to tell you I finally said to God: I want to thank You and praise You for my marriage just the way it is. I want to thank You and praise You for my husband just the way he is. Later I got the teaching, and would like to give it to you.

When I was a little girl I wanted to be a nun. My mother wasn't a Catholic. She had been baptized as a Christian. No one took me by the hand. I guess I wasn't suppose to be a nun. I grew up, and married. But always there was this part in here that hurt. I didn't know what it was. I loved my husband. I loved my children. I wondered, what was wrong with me because I didn't become a nun. There always was this space that was hurting.

In the sixties, when I had the surgery, the doctors said that they didn't know how I was living. How I even had children. When I had the operation I was brought back during the operation. I had already been out of the body. Through His love I was brought back. I still hurt because Jesus was there in Heaven and I'm back here on earth.

That's when I became a mystic. Anyway I've had priests tell me that God didn't call me to be a doormat. I felt like a doormat emotionally, you know what I'm talking about. I was told that it's ok to separate. I wouldn't be a doormat without God's permission. Therefore I'm going to thank and praise Him for my situation the way it is.

Then one day, I turned on "Mother Angela". There was going to be a priest on there who had a near-death-out-of - the-body experience. I had never heard a priest testify on this topic.

The story was that he was out west. He had a head-on collision with a vehicle. He was sent to the hospital and he had a broken neck. All the churches in the community were praying for him. He recovered enough to move about. He had to wear a Halo brace. It included two screws in his head and the brace.

In time he recovered enough to go back and pray mass. He was praying Mass that day when suddenly the Scriptures became enlarged and illuminated. He said to himself, "What is happening to me?" He also said that he managed to get through the Mass, went back to the rectory, and drank cup after cup of coffee. He kept saying, "What just happened to me?"

He said, "I always thought that I had an excuse for whatever I did. I would say Lord, he or she made me do it. But I realized, *when you stand before the truth, it's just you and God.* Nobody makes you do it.

Yes Lord, I did that.

Yes Lord, I said that.

He said that my sentence was hell. He said, yes Jesus I deserve that. And then there was this silence and He heard a woman's voice saying, "Let's give him more time."

Then Jesus said, "He is going to be a priest all these years for his self, mother and not for me."

"If we give him more grace," she said.

And there was a silence and Jesus said, "Mother he is yours."

Then the priest said, "I've been hers ever since."

The Scripture he was reading was the story of the vine dresser. An owner came into the field and saw a tree that was not bearing fruit. The owner said, "Cut it down and throw it into the fire."

The vine dresser said, "Sir, let me give it more time. Let me hoe around that tree. Let me fertilize that tree and if it does not bear, then I will cut it down."

I saw my life in this parable. See, God used my husband to fertilize this tree to bear fruit. To prepare this tree so I couldn't blame my husband anymore. I realized that he was a gift from God that was preparing me to do what God wanted me to do.

I wanted to give you this teaching.

7.16 Radio, Jesus and Mother Mary

Since my out-of-body-near-death experience I had fallen in love with Jesus in another dimension. I was riding along in a car and decided to turn the radio on. Then I heard in my head a voice, it said, "Don't turn the outside in."

I turned the radio off. Then I'm worshiping Jesus and I'm singing.

Then the voice said, "Be still."

I thought, God wants us to praise Him. The Scripture says that God inhabits the praises of His people. So I kept on singing.

Then I heard, "Be still."

I thought that this was just psychological, I'm just imaging this. So I kept on singing. You can't make yourself stop thinking. Then I was stopped, not with my tongue, just inside.

So I said to Jesus, "I'm sorry."

Then this is what I heard very strong come into my head, "My child, tell all my people to love My Mother. Tell my people to love My Mother. For I will go before you. I will engineer the circumstances. Tell my people to love My Mother."

I started to cry and I said, "Lord, how will I do that, because it takes away from You to do that," I heard, "My child, you tell them that God is love. When they love My Mother, it is God's love."

That night when I was saying my prayers, this is what I said to Jesus, "Lord Jesus, if You're telling me to tell Your people to love Your Mother, I don't know if I love her."

Then I said, "Lord Jesus, would you teach me to love Your Mother as You love her. Would You teach me to know her as You know her.

Lord Jesus would you teach me to be more like Your Mother." Nobody knew that I prayed that. So what happened?

I started getting these teachings. I began to learn about her, and it has not stopped yet!

7.17 A Mother's Heart Is Warm Indeed

We had two state troopers, many, many years ago that were shot in our little town of Berkeley Springs. They were looking for some offender.
When they found him, he came out shooting and killed them both.

Both of the state troopers had a wife.

Both of the state troopers had a son.

Both of the state troopers had a mother.

I'm at the sink the next morning and I was happily singing. All of a sudden I stopped and said, "God, how come I have all this joy, with all this sadness about. I feel guilty that I am happy."

Then I heard, "Because my child, your joy will be in Me, as the darkness gets darker."

I didn't know about spiritual darkness covering the earth. This was many years ago.

Then I heard, "I'm going to give you a new poem today."

I guess because I was happy and singing, this was going to be a happy poem. I picked up a pen, papers were in front of me, and I started to cry.

I wrote this poem through tears, and this is what I heard from Jesus.

> My mother's heart is warm indeed
>   She takes Me to her side
> And folds her gentle arms about
>   She is My Father's guide

In her My Father placed this life
        And blessed Me in Her womb
Her heart so broken went with Me
        upon the cross and to the tomb

What joy was hers that blessed day
        I rose up from the grave
To bring the proof that I am He
        who came to heal and save

O mother, mother at My side
        You're always there with Me
And honor will be yours someday
        The world sees Me with Thee

My Father loves my blessed mother
        He planned her out of love
The message sent to her from Him
        Was "blessed" from above

Thank you Father for Your words
        That never pass away
And blessed for all generations
        mean words for us today

Dear mother of each Father's child
        Your plan in life's the same
So walk with me as mother did
        And love will be a flame

Then winds can blow and storms arise
        And earth can rock and shake
But nothing can put out that flame
        Because your hand in Mine I'll take

When I was finished, He told me why I was crying. He said, "I just let you feel the heart of the mothers who just lost their sons. I just let you feel the heart of mothers who have sons to raise now without their earthly fathers. I just let you feel the heart of a mother whose boy was shot. My Mother felt all these."

Jesus let me now that the Blessed Mother feels every heart. She won't judge people by what they are, were or did. She is a mother, she loves them all from a mother's heart.

I just wanted to share that with you.

7.18 Special Water, Holy Ground

What is interesting about Berkeley Springs is George Washington's Bathtub. George Washington came here for the waters. The Indians came from all around for that spring. There they didn't fight. They called that area Holy Ground. In fact a lot of the highway routes were at one time Indian paths.

Many people have come to that spring. Franklin Delanore Roosevelt, because he had polio was responsible for building our hospital. It was originally called the "Pines". It was built for crippled children. That is how it originated. Later its name was changed to the "War Memorial" hospital.

Do you think that it is a coincidence that the Bethesda Naval hospital, when you go into the rotunda there are pictures of Franklin and Eleanor Roosevelt lining the walls. I wondered, why are these pictures here? Then I found out, because the hospital was built during his term of office.

Is it a coincidence that in the Bible the pool that they dipped people in for healing was called Bethesda?

I wanted to tell you that.

7.19 Trinity Project, Mary's Protection

My Uncle Sam was the engineer for the Trinity Project. When they tested the first atomic bomb they named that test Trinity. Did you know that? I have a lot of records on my Uncle. He worked with all of the important people on the project.

I'm going to give you a mystical teaching. It always bothered me about the atomic bomb. But I didn't know how Our Lady was involved.

A lady who lives in Oklahoma told me this story. When the atomic bomb was being tested one of her lady friends had a vision in a dream. The lady saw Our Lady over the mushroom cloud with her hands extended down and rays extending from her hands.

What I wanted to tell you is that it bothered me that my uncle was the engineer on the project. I thought it was something terrible. Of course some good has come out of all this. For example, atomic energy to power electric generating plants and transportation.

It bothered me for a long time until I got the teachings. You see, when the Japanese bombed Pearl Harbor on December 7th, it was the eve of the Feast of the Immaculate Conception. The peace treaty was signed on August 15th, the Feast of the Assumption. The Japanese surrendered when we dropped the bomb on Hiroshima and it saved many American lives. I began to see that Our Lady was protecting us even though it seemed awful.

Why did they choose July 16th, 1945, the Feast of our Lady of Mt. Carmel to test the bomb? They didn't drop it from an airplane. They constructed a tower to hold it prior to detonation. As I was researching it, I found out that they didn't know just what would happen when they tested the bomb. They were prepared for all kinds of possibilities.

They had doctors available in the adjacent towns and all kinds of emergency people ready to go.

When the bomb was ready to be tested it rained. It rained so hard that they couldn't test. It rained for a couple of days. Then on July 16th the rain stopped and they detonated the bomb. The rain had saved the area!

Now here we go! In the Old Testament, they needed rain. Elijah said, "Let's go up on Mt. Carmel."

All the different leaders and priests called on their gods for rain and nothing happened. Check it out in the Bible.

Elijah said, "Build an altar, dig a trench around the altar, soak the sacrifice and the wood. Fill the trench with water."

Elijah then called on God and fire came from Heaven and consumed the sacrifice. It then began to rain and rain.

Then I'm thinking, prior to the bomb test, it rained and the rain saved the area. Our Lady had saved us!

Interesting?

7.20 Our Lady of La Salette Statue in Berkeley Springs   Story by John Gruber

I was in the hospital in Georgetown University and a candy striper came up, and asked, "Do you want a book?"

I said, "Sure I'll take a book." I thought that was the best way to get rid of her. So I took a book. The next day I opened the book up. It was a Reader's Digest condensed version of different stories. I had opened it up to a story about Our Lady of La Salette.

Five years later I figured that it is time to get a statue. At that time we had signs for the Catholic church on every road coming into Berkeley Springs. I was sure that my house was a good spot for the statue.

I located a statue in Altamont, New York. The priest said, "We are getting a new statue for our grounds and the old one will be available." It took six to eight months before it was ready to go up. It was in the winter time and I had to wait for spring. In the meantime the foundation and pedestal were constructed.

The statue weighed 800 to 900 pounds. He said, "When you come up, we'll have a crane here to set it on your truck."

I said, "Ok."

A man loaned me his truck and I went up to get the statue. I brought it back, backed the truck right up to the foundation and it was a perfect fit! The statue slid right off the truck and onto the foundation. All I needed to use was a come-along.

It seemed like Our Lord was in charge.

Our Lady of La Salette appeared to two children in the mountains of France in 1846. The children were returning from their duties of tending the cows on Mount Sous-Les Baisses. They saw a beautiful lady weeping. She then spoke to them in French even as she wept. She was clothed in a white robe. Her head was buried in her hands and she wore a headdress of roses. She wanted people to respect the name of God, and she also said, "Very well my children, make this known to all my people."

Story told by John Gruber. Photos by John Gruber. Statue located on the hill at the top of Fairfax street.

Dedication of the statue of Our Lady of La Salette

7.21 Saint Nicholas

Every year I put up our Christmas tree in our second dining room in front of Our Lady of Lourdes. There is a shelf and I take down Bernadette and put up Santa Claus kneeling over the crib of the baby Jesus in the manger.

I was thinking, how many times we hear the song, "Away in the manger, no crib for a bed...the little Lord Jesus asleep on the hay."

Jesus was born in a cave. They were natural shelters for animals in the winter. "There was no place in the inn." So Jesus was born in a cave for animals. He was laid in the trough which holds the animals' food.

In the nativity scene you always see Jesus laying in the hay. So we have the statue of Santa Claus kneeling before Jesus in a manger. I thought I would explain to people why it's like that.

We have young people come in and I say to them and the adults too, "Do you know where Santa Claus originates from?"

They think it is the North Pole. So I decided I would teach them some stories. Because they have never heard some of the more true stories.

This story starts with Nicholas. Many years ago I saw a beautiful movie for children. I am child-like so I enjoyed it. It was the story of Saint Nicholas. Nicholas was a Bishop. He had a great devotion to the infant Jesus. In his cathedral where he said Mass, he took a statue of the baby Jesus and laid it in a manger in his church. He would bow down and adore the baby Jesus. This was symbolic for his people.

The land was being devastated. It was during the time when people were put in prison for their faith. Nicholas was put in prison for years. While he was there they burnt his church. When he came out of the prison he was an old man. That is why he is shown with a beard. He went into his town and he heard music coming from his rebuilt church. When he entered the church, the priest that was saying Mass was the little boy who was an altar boy when Nicholas was a priest.

Nicholas found out that when they burned the church, the little boy had run into the church and saved the statue of the infant Jesus. The same statue is in their manger in church.

Now I'm going to tell you another story of Santa Claus. It begins with Nicholas, who was born in the third century in the village of Patra. At the time the area was Greek. It is now on the southern coast of Turkey.

His devout parents who raised him to be a devout Christian died in an epidemic when Nicholas was still young. Obeying Jesus' words, "To sell your possessions and give the money to the poor," Nicholas used his entire inheritance to assist the needy, the sick and the suffering.

He dedicated his life to serving God. He was made the Bishop of Myra when he was a young man. Bishop Nicholas became known through-out the land for his generosity to those in need, his love for children and his concern for sailors and ships.

Under the Roman Dioclesan, who ruthlessly persecuted Christians, Nicholas suffered for his faith. He was exiled and imprisoned. The prisons were so full of bishops, priests and deacons that there was no room for the real criminals, murders, thieves and robbers. After his release, Nicholas attended the church of Nicea in 325. He died on December 343 in Myra and was buried in his cathedral church.

After his burial a unique relic called manna formed on his grave. This substance was said to have healing powers. Therefore it fostered the growth of devotion to Nicholas.

The anniversary of his death became the day of his celebration. Saint Nicholas day is December 6th.

Through the centuries many stories and legends have been told about Saint Nicholas' life and deeds. These accounts help us to understand his extraordinary character and why he is so beloved and revered as protector and helper of those in need.

I thought I would tell this because young people know about Santa Claus but they don't know Saint Nicholas. This is the spiritual side of Santa Claus.

7.22   Eucharistic Miracle at Lanciano

Today I would like to speak about the Holy Eucharist and what it really is. When I was at Mass this morning there was a sermon on the Holy Eucharist. It was about the scripture when Jesus was going towards John the Baptist. John the Baptist said, "Behold the Lamb of God." He saw Jesus but called him the Lamb of God. What is the Lamb of God?

Jesus said, "This bread I will give is My Flesh for the life of the world."

In 1984 I was privileged to go to Italy. We rented a van and drove from Rome across the country to a little town called Lanciano, where a Eucharist miracle took place in the eight century. It is a story about a priest who had a Eucharistic miracle.

It was also interesting to learn when I was there how the town got its name. The tradition handed down was that the soldier who pierced the side of Jesus on the cross to prove that Jesus was dead was Longinus. Longinus became a great Christian. Tradition has it that he went to that area and

Lanciano was named for him. Because he was the one that put the lance in the side of Jesus.

We experienced something there and this is the story.

It's the story about a priest that at the moment of consecration had doubts. He said to himself, "Is this really the Body and Blood of Jesus Christ?"

> It still looks like blood.
> It still looks like wine.
> Is it real?

When his doubts came, a miracle happened. The sacred host turned into flesh in his very hands. The wine in the chalice turned into blood at that moment.

It has been kept all these years with no preservatives. 1,200 years later it is still intact. We had the privilege of going there, going into the church, going in behind the tabernacle and there you could witness it. You can see the sacred host, which is human flesh and blood.

In fact if you ever go to Maria's Garden, we have above the door going into the Garden dining room a plaque from there.

The word Eucharist means thanksgiving. In 1971 and again in 1981, the church allowed a university in Italy to do research on the holy relics. They discovered that the flesh is a piece of the human heart. The blood type is identical as to what is in that heart's flesh. The blood has coagulated into five parts. I could see little holes in the coagulated blood and I asked my doctor about that. He said the holes would be formed when the oxygen leaves.

In order to test this blood it would have to be only one day old. When it was tested it had the same properties of normal fresh serum.

I thanked God for letting me see with my eyes which I believed by faith. We have the freedom to go to Holy Communion to receive Jesus' Body and Blood whenever we wish to. Jesus gives us a heart transplant when we receive Holy Communion.

Jesus instituted the Holy Eucharist at the Last Supper. He said, "It is better for you that I go. For if I didn't leave you the Spirit couldn't come to you."

Now He is with you but He shall be in you.

Then He took the bread and wine and blessed it. He said, "This is My Flesh."

Then He took the cup of wine and blessed it saying, "This is My Blood of the New and Everlasting Covenant, and lo I am with you till the end of time."

7.23 Maria's Garden, Far and Wide

One day a man was looking around in the restaurant and I asked him, "How did you hear about Maria's Garden?"

He said, "A nun in the Vatican told me about it."

In 1983, in Portugal, my son Curtis was on a bus talking to a lady.

She asked, "Where are you from?"

He said, "From a little place in West Virginia."

She said, "I heard that in West Virginia there is a restaurant with icons of the Blessed Mother."

He said, "Maria's Garden?"

She said, "Yes."

He said, "Here, would you like a brochure?"

7.24 The Lady of the New Advent

I found a pamphlet describing visions of George Washington. In it George Washington said that he witnessed this vision and then the vision began to fade and then he last saw nothing but rising curling vapors. Then standing before him was the mysterious visitor he had first beheld.

He said to me, "Son of the Republic, what you have seen is to be interpreted. There are three great perils that will come upon the Republic. The most fearful is the third. The third peril is dependent upon Divine Assistance. The whole world will unite against the Republic but will not prevail."

George Washington said that he thought that he had seen a vision of the progress and destiny of the United States.

I had on the wall an icon, called "The Lady of the New Advent". I have since put it on the wall in the front lobby. It was commissioned by the Archdiocese of Denver, Colorado to celebrate the Third Millennium. This is the Age of the Spirit, it will reveal Mary.

In 1988 in Russia was the commemoration of 1000 years of Christianity. In 1988 is when the Archbishop of Colorado commemorated the Lady of the New Advent.

7.25   U. S. A. and the Immaculate Conception

Did you know that the Mississippi River was originally called the "River of the Immaculate Conception" and the Chesapeake Bay was called "The Bay of the Mother of God"? All of the rivers of the U.S.A. were originally travelled by priests, Spanish and French Catholic explorers.

George Washington was very Christian. He respected the name of Jesus. In 1776 he told his troops not to violate the Holy Name of Jesus. They would be reprimanded by both him and God. He said grace before every meal. He used the Sign of the Cross. He had a picture of Mary in his house. His mother's name was Mary. When he was dying in 1799 he sent for a Jesuit priest. He was first in war, first in peace and first in the hearts of his country men.

A shrine of the Immaculate Conception was built in Washington, D. C. It was built for all the legislators of the U. S. A. who wished to know to who the supernatural forces of our country belonged.

7.26 The Tear Drop Memorial

There are a lot of things we don't learn about Russia in the media. Why do we hear and say the Holy Mother of Russia? At a public forum their president, Vladimir Putin stated that the West denies their Christian roots and the Christian Holidays are abolished. It is even known that Gorbachev was a Christian.

Someone who had been a guest at Maria's Garden sent me this information. I never knew of this or had ever heard about it. It is a sculpture by the Russian Artist Zurab Tsereteli. It is a gift from the Russian government to the United States of America as a memorial to the 9/11 victims. The sculpture is located in Bayonne, New Jersey.

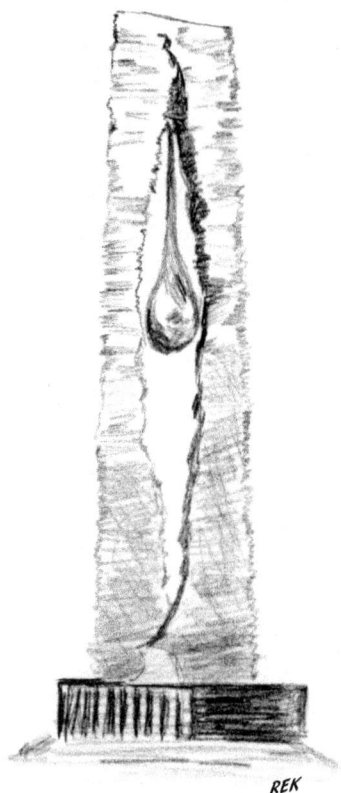
REK

This beautiful, impressive memorial is a 100 feet high bronze clad tower. It has a jagged split in the center and in this hangs a 40 foot long nickel coated teardrop. On the bottom of the base the marble has names of the people who lost their lives.

The ground breaking took place in September of 2005 and was attended by the President of Russia. A year later it was dedicated in a ceremony by the U. S. president.

7.27 Our Lady, Queen of Peace, Statue

This is how I learned about this. My brother worked in Delaware in a corporate office. One day in 1982 he called me and said, "The Blessed Mother is looking in the window of my third floor office." Next to his office was the place where the sculpture Charles C. Parks and the City of Wilmington had it exhibited. This was in Rodney square. After some time it was sent off to its home in Santa Clara, California.

I had to see this, so I went up to visit him and viewed this fantastic and beautiful statue. It is so large that I only came up to the top of its toe.

This 8,400 pound statue is 33 feet high. It is made of stainless steel. It is of the Blessed Mother with outstretched arms. Some time later in 1998 another statue was commissioned, built and sent up to Chicago.

The last one was built in 2000 for the parish Holy Spirit Catholic Church in New Castle, Delaware. The only difference in this one is that the face was designed after Our Lady of Medjugorje.

Isn't That Interesting!

7.28 Our Lady of the Milk

A few yards down from the Church of the Nativity in Bethlehem is another church. It is called Our Lady of the Milk Grotto.

You see, Jesus was born in a cave. In that cave were different passage ways. When Our Lady nursed the baby Jesus she would go into a section all to herself. In that section all of the rocks turned white. When the Franciscans took over the holy land, they took some of these rocks and they were exported all over the world.

The first shrine to Our Lady is in St. Augustine, Florida. Outside the old town of St. Augustine is a walkway that goes into the woods. There is a little chapel there and in that chapel is a statue of Mary. Mary is nursing the baby Jesus. The name of that chapel is Our Lady of La Leche (milk).

This was also the first city in this country, and was founded by the Spanish. This *is* the land flowing with milk and honey.

The Milk Grotto in Bethlehem was built by St. Paula and when women become pregnant they go there and pray for good milk for their babies.

7.29 The Song, "The Miracle of the Rosary"

This is about the song that Elvis Presley sings, "The Miracle of the Rosary". In the song he asks Mary to pray for sinners. I have prayed for Elvis for many years.

The story starts with Delores Hart. She was Elvis's leading lady in a movie. One time they were out west in a hotel, and he comes into her room reading scripture. He was very religious. Later she became a nun. She is a mother superior in a convent.

You know that the pope put a blessing on all who were involved in the making of that song.

This is how I first found out about that song. I was riding in a car in the back seat with a lady I didn't know. We were going to the Shrine of Our Lady of Fatima in Washington, New Jersey. She said that she had heard the most beautiful song about the rosary the other day. It was on an album by Elvis Presley. In my head I'm thinking, God, I would like to hear that.

We got to the shrine. Busses were there from all over. The man and lady leading the music ministry that day were Lee and Mary Denson. After it was finished, you could buy their album. I went down to the visitor's center and am buying their album. I told Mr. Denson about the lady who told me about the song, *The Miracle of the Rosary* by Elvis Presley.

He said, "Oh, I taught that to him."

He said that he grew up with Elvis. He was an early rockabilly music performer and the person who taught Elvis to play guitar when he was 13. Elvis' and Lee's families attended the same church in Memphis in 1948. Lee is the one that wrote the song. I bought the album. On the back was this story. Lee and Mary were night club entertainers. She

Isn't That Interesting!

was Catholic, he was not. She had lost her rosary. She left the room temporarily. When she came back, on her bed laying there was her rosary. When Lee came home she told him about it and they decided to pray.

The next day they were in church in Massachusetts and three times in his homily the priest said "The Blessed Mother performs many miracles for us and we don't appreciate it." They mentioned it to some parishioners and they didn't hear it. Then they mentioned it to the priest and he said that he never mentioned it. The priest said that he could have been the instrument in which it was presented to them.

That night Lee was awakened with a strong impulse to write the song. It came to him unusually fast as he wrote it, *The Miracle of the Rosary*. Lee went on to California where he became a Catholic.

In 1968 at a prayer meeting with the archbishop of Panama present, three times they played that song and each time the entire room was filled with the fragrance of roses. That became Lee's favorite song. That is the story behind *The Miracle of the Rosary*.

7.30 Edgar Allen Poe

In a book of my grandfathers I found a poem by Edgar Allen Poe. It was called *Hymn*. In this poem one of the lines said, "Mother of God be with me still." It is about Edgar Allen Poe and he is praying to Our Lady.

So what is interesting, I got curious about Edgar Allen Poe. A priest told me a story that many years ago a man collapsed on the steps of his church. Passerbys thought that he was some old drunk and they ignored him. But the priest went out and he found out that the man was ill.

He then found out that the man was Edgar Allen Poe. He was taken to the hospital and later died.

I'm thinking, "Baltimore." I got real curious and went to the encyclopedia to look up Edgar Allen Poe. I wanted to see if he died on the steps of a Catholic church. He did.

Well, guess what I discovered. Edgar Allen Poe had many aliases. As a young man he was sent to England to a boarding school. There he went by the name of William Wilson. He wrote a story called *William Wilson*. In this boarding school were two William Wilsons. One was very good and one was very bad. The bad one didn't like the good one. In the story they either went up the stairs or down the stairs. Also in the story the bad one destroyed the good one. That is the short story of William Wilson.

I told this to my son. He said, "Mom, in college I did a report on the story of Edgar Allen Poe's *William Wilson*. It was Edgar Allen Poe's biography. In his life he either went up or he went down.

Do you think that it was a coincidence that the man who founded AA was a man by the name of Bill Wilson? Also when I looked it up in the encyclopedia, I found out that one of the names Poe went by was Perry. I said, "Oh God, that is my name!"

Edgar Allen Poe was bipolar and back then they didn't understand it. In that poem *Hymn*, he called out to Our Lady.

He also wrote *The Raven*. This is what is interesting about *The Raven*. A raven fed Elijah. A raven was the first bird sent out of Noah's ark. There are a lot of spiritual connotations in Poe's work.

I just wanted to tell you that.

7.31 One Day

Peg was telling a teaching:
She said, "One day a lady and man were sitting at one of the tables and I came in."
The lady asked, "Do you own this place?"
I answered, "No, God does, and I work for Him."
The lady then said, "Do you know that there is a glowing light all around you!"
Peg told us, "I don't know what that is. Could it be that I go to Mass every day and it's the Holy Eucharist?"
She answered, "You have the Holy Spirit within you. You emit a Holy Light, the Light of God."
Peg said, "I feel that I'm doing God's work. Some day I may be able to step back and God will take over."

7.32 Lazarus

I looked up the word Lazarus. The meaning of the word Lazarus means "God is help". Not "God help me", but "God is help", and I went, "I never knew that!"
I wondered, why in the Scriptures did they name that poor beggar Lazarus?
The Statue of Liberty in the United States of America is a statue of a woman holding a book and a torch. On the book is written 1776. At the foot of the Statue of Liberty is a plaque. On it is inscribed a sonnet entitle New Colossus. This was written for a fundraiser auction to raise money for the pedestal the Statue of Liberty sits on.
A famous phrase from it is, "Give me your tired, your poor, your huddled masses yearning to breathe free."
This sonnet was written by a lady, Emma Lazarus.

7.33 Russian Conversion Continued

At Fatima our Lady has said to pray for the conversion of Russia.

> On May 13, 1991, John Paul goes to Fatima to worship.
> Aug 18, 19, 20, 1991 Gorbachev is put under house arrest.
> December 8, Feast of the Immaculate Conception. The paper to dissolve the Soviet Union was signed.
> December 25,1991, The Soviet flag comes down and the Russian flag goes up.

Gorbachev was baptized as a baby. He was consecrated to Mother Mary by his mother. So was Putin. He was baptized as a baby. His mother put him at the foot of Mary's statue. I believe that she is going to work through him for the conversion of Russia.

It's already happening. The walls fell. The Russians are in the international Space Station. They sent an icon of Our Lady of Kazan up to the space station and it is there now. Putin is seen as kissing the icon of The Lady of Kazan. In Russia, prayer is now being put back into the schools. It is against the law to have an abortion. It is against the law for same sex marriage.

It never came to me until the other day, the first priest to receive all of the orders of priesthood in the United States was Demetrius Gallitzen. Prince Gallitzen was a Russian prince. He changed his name to Father Smith. Think of it! The first priest to become a priest in the United States was a Russian prince. What do you think of it?

I just wanted to tell you that.

7.34 Three Icons & St. John Neumann

Many years ago, while Maria's Garden was coming together, this main dining room that we are sitting in now was still an outside yard. I went to an Irish auction at our church. At this auction on a table were three icons in black frames. One was our Lord, one was the Holy Mother and the other one was St. John of Nepomucene.

While I'm looking at these three icons, I was looking at St. John of Nepomucene. I'm hearing, St. John Neumann.

As I was bidding for them, I looked over and the lady that was biding against me, I knew. I leaned over and said, "I need these for the restaurant." She said, "Oh, sure, sure." She quit bidding and I ended up getting the three icons. I brought them down to the second dining room at the end of the building. I had them laying on the table and this man came in and began eating.

He said, "That is not St. John Neumann."

I said, "Who is he?"

He said, "St. John of Nepomucene."

I said, "Who was he Rudy?"

Rudy who was Czechoslovakian, said, "He was the confessor to the queen. When the king asked him to reveal the queens confession, he said no and he was killed. They threw him in the river and he drowned. Then a bright light hung out over the spot where they threw him into the river. Today he is know as the Patron Saint of the Confessional."

Do you think it was a coincidence that St. John Neumann was named after him?

One day a lady came in and brought me a relic of St. John Neumann. In the Shrine of the Immaculate Conception in Washington, D.C., there is a chapel on the lower level. It is St. John Neumann's Chapel, the confessional chapel for Our Lady's Shrine.

7.35 Mr. Fusek

Mr. Fusek grew up to be a very important man in Czechoslovakia. He had his own electronics company, was a member of parliament and a representative to the Vatican. His assets were over 60 million dollars.

When his land was being invaded, twice he was called in. But money talks and he was sent home. That time his wife had sat outside the building all night long praying for him. The third time he was called in a person told him, "Mr. Fusek don't go home, they are going to kill you."

So Mr. Fusek fled his country with his family with nothing but the clothes on his back. They came to the United States as refugees. Now as he was leaving, his brother told him to take the gold coins Mr. Fusek had given him. He said, "They will help you on your way."

Mr. Fusek said, "No, I gave them to you."

As they fled, they came to a little town with an inn. Mr. Fusek said to the innkeeper, "Sir my wife and I are so tired. May we have a cup of tea?"

As he said this his hand was laying on his chest and he touched something in his pocket. His brother had slipped the gold coins in his pocket. That helped them get on their way.

Mr. Fusek could get no employment. Then he noticed that common laborers got work. He filled out another work employment record that said he was a carpenter's helper. He got a job in New York at St. Patrick's Church.

He said that it was hard to do repairs because someone was always in the church praying. So he set his alarm for two in the morning. He was working on a set of stairs and he heard a voice say, "Who's hammering?" It was the Bishop. This was a connecting point. It later came out in an article.

Mr. Fusek's daughter was being given an award by the Queen of England. It mentioned the parent's name. The Bishop saw that and went in to where Mr. Fusek was working and said, "Mr. Fusek, why didn't you tell me who you where? I have some place that I want to put you."

He put him at the Shrine of the Immaculate Conception in Washington D.C., Our Lady's National Shrine.

7.36 The Shrine of the Immaculate Conception, The Czech Chapel

In all those years the pillars in the lower crypt of the Shrine had many Czech names on them but there was no Czech chapel. When Saint John Neumann was canonized, he was from Bohemia. Then they received the beginning of the funding for the St. John Neumann Chapel, which would be the Czech chapel.

In that chapel there is a statue of Our Lady holding the Baby Jesus. The lightning bolts coming down from it represent this miracle!; this is the confessional Chapel.

7.37 St. Apollinaris and the Apollo Moon Mission

Jully 20th is the Feast Day of St. Apollinaris. Most people don't know who St. Apollinaris is. St. Apollinaris was made a bishop by St. Peter. It is kind of interesting because his feast day was originally January 8, but in 1969 the calendar for this date for America was changed to July 20th.

I think that it's rather providential because in 1969 America departed to the moon on July 16th. This was the anniversary of the Feast of Our Lady of Mt. Carmel. They landed on the moon on July 20th. That was the Feast day of St. Apollinaris and it was called the Apollo Mission.

The first words that they said were, "The Eagle has landed."

America was the first to land on the moon.

I think that it's rather providential, because if you check the records, you will find that the first elements taken to the moon were bread and wine. Buzz Aldrin's religion was Presbyterian and he had permission to take a little container of bread and wine to the moon.

So the first elements on the moon were bread and wine and the first words spoken were, "The Eagle has landed."

7.38 The Body of Christ

July 20, 1977, is the Feast Day of St. Apollinaris. In Kansas City, Kansas, a meeting called the Catholic Charismatic Conference was held. All denominations met. Cardinal Suenens was sent by Pope Paul VI to oversee it.

In the program it said we can pray together, but on Sunday morning we went to our separated places of worship. We were not one in the Celebration of the Holy Eucharist and you could feel the separation of the parts. There was a message that night that went, "Mourn and weep, for the Body of My Son is broken."

After the message was spoken 55,000 people in Arrowhead Stadium fell to their knees and wept.

I looked up to the sky that night and I wept, "Dear God, here in the heart of our nation the Holy Spirit is weeping for the healing of the Body of Christ."

That is when I came back and was given this poem:

The Body of Christ
These arms and legs all made by God
Are joined by many parts
That work together from within
And nourished by our hearts

Some hidden parts we never see
Are working just the same
If broken they can't function
A leg could then be lame

It could affect their hearts and sight
And useless we'd soon be.
But God would send someone to care
For you're His property

Yet Jesus came from God above
To live within our hearts
And give this body His great love
That cares for all these parts

God's plan for man does far exceed
The reason of our mind
He wants our body to be whole
So let's not look behind

Now try to put your thoughts ahead
To see just how we're made
For every broken arm or leg
A healing price was paid

God's love for us was in His Son
Who came to show the way
Just as He did in years gone by
To Noah in his day

So Jesus came to build His church
An ark to enter in
The door is open to each child
The fee, repent of sin

A body of redeemed His church
Of this, we now are part
But this can only be accomplished
By those who have His Heart

I Corinthians 12:12-30 is a poem the Lord spoke to me. He showed me a broken body. The Church is the body of Christ. Yet Jesus' body was never broken. (John 19:31) God made everything to be whole and within everybody there is a healing.

If a bone is broken, a doctor can set the bones in place but the healing takes place when the bones are joined and the body is healing. If the bones are joined at the wrong place when the bones knit together, the body will be crippled.

We are living in a time when the church, (the Body of Christ) has been broken since the reformation. This poem (arms and legs represent denominations and divisions) describes the body of Christ. Jesus never planted a broken church. Man has separated His Body which is One-The Church.

As I am writing this I begin to see the more man breaks His bones (His Church) the more He suffers and Our Blessed Mother suffers. Because no mother can see her son suffer without pain.

7.39 The Bones Coming Together to Be One

God showed me that a doctor can set the bones but he can't heal them. Healing takes place when the bones are touching long enough. But the knitting that brings the parts together will be the heart that pumps the blood. It knits all the parts together and that will be the Holy Eucharist.

It is interesting in Corinthians, St. Paul was saying "There's scandal in the church. You are divided. Some say, I belong to Paul; some say, I belong to Peter; and some say, I belong to Apollis. (I thought it was some Greek god). There is only one crucified Christ, and you are separating Him. It's a scandal."

In the Old Testament, God said to Ezekiel, "Look out over this vast desert, there's many bones. They are separate, they are dry." He said, "Prophesy to these bones. and tell the bones to come together." God said, "I will put flesh, and I will put sinew, and I will bring spirit."

They set up and became a very strong nation. God said, "This is the whole house of Israel. Now I will take the stick of Judah and the stick of Joseph and I will make them one stick in my hand. They will be no longer two nations, but one nation with one king over them all."

I see the church as the new Israel. The two sticks that God brings together, Israel the old and Israel the new. But how He brings it together is in the blood line. You see, the blood that is passed through is from the mother's side. Once a Jew, always a Jew. It is Jewish blood that flows through their veins. Mary was a Jewish virgin. But the Immaculate Conception was placed in St. Ann. She was of the tribe of Judah.

I think it's interesting, in the New Testament, who opens the scrolls? The Lion of the tribe of Judah is Jesus Christ. In Maria's Garden there is a huge painting. It shows our Lord King sitting on a throne. The throne represents America. At His feet are two lions. Then I realized why there are two lions at His feet. One is the Lion of the tribe of Judah, Old Testament and the other is the Lion of the tribe of Judah, New Testament.

God took on human flesh in a Jewish virgin. That blood line that flowed into our Lord's veins was Jewish blood of Judah. When we receive Him in the Holy Eucharist, Jewish blood flows into our veins.

I wanted to tell you that.

7.40 George Washington and the New Advent

All these years I've been teaching about George Washington and the vision he had at Valley Forge in 1777. He was given a vision of the birth, progress and destiny of the United States of America.

I found and ordered a reproduction pamphlet telling about this vision. The story had originally appeared in the *National Tribute* in 1880. The pamphlet was called *The Vision of George Washington*.

It begins with the last time I saw Antony Sherman. He was in Independence Square, Pennsylvania. He said that he was going to tell about Washington's vision. You know that most people don't know this story. I think that this is interesting because we're here on Independence Street.

A single beautiful female figure came before him. She said, "Son of the Republic, learn and listen. These are the three perils that will befall the world." I had forgot that I had these pamphlets about George Washington's vision. Well, the other day the cleaning lady Cordelia, was cleaning out a closet and found the pamphlets. I went, "Oh thank you. I have been wanting to share that with people."

I got the pamphlets out and when I came to the back page, it begins: "The scene began to fade and I last saw nothing but the rising circling vapor I had first beheld. This at once disappeared and I saw myself before the mysterious visitor who in the same voice I had heard before say, "Son of the Republic, what you have just seen is thus interpreted: Three great perils will come upon the Republic. We have already gone before the first two horrible trials. The most fearful is the third, in which the whole world united against her will fail. Let every child of the Republic learn to live for his God, His land and the Union." With these words the

Vision vanished, I got up from my seat and I thought I had seen a vision of the birth, progress and destiny of the United States."

"Such my friend," said the narrator, "Were the words I heard from Washington's lips and America would do well to profit by them."

Then I said, "Wait a minute God, you told me that many years ago. Many years ago I was at home and in a split second I had this knowledge: In the first period of time it was the Time of God the Father. Two thousand years ago it was the Time of God the Son. Now You're coming as a triumphal third period, the Time of the Spirit. The Holy Spirit will reveal Mary."

I remember thinking, "God," and I asked this priest, "How is it possible to have all the knowledge on a certain topic in a split second?"

He said, "That is called infused wisdom."

That was many years ago and I never picked up on it. In my poetry book I have a poem *As The Age Draws Nigh*. Nigh does not mean the end of everything. Nigh means about to come forth. This triumphal third period is the Time of The Triumph of Mary. The Age of the Spirit will reveal Mary.

I went, "Wait a minute God." When it talks about the Second Advent, over in that room there is an icon, I have had it for years. The title of it is, *The Lady of the New Advent*. It was commissioned by the Archdiocese of Denver, Colorado in 1988 to celebrate the coming of the Third Advent of Christianity. We have had it all along but I never connected it.

I just wanted to tell that this icon is at Maria's Garden.

Copies of General Washington's Vision may be obtained from:
Old Paths Tract Society, Inc., Shoals, Ind. 47581

8   Paintings, Statues, Pictures & Icons

Maria's Garden is also a product of the wonderful gifts that her guests, patrons and friends from all walks of life, different religions and all parts of the world have given to the Inn. These religious articles make Maria's Garden "one of a kind". It will touch your heart as you become overwhelmed looking at all the very interesting donations that have been given.

Special painting commissioned for
Father Salazar's Book, *The True Believer.*

Here the publisher, Bob and his wife Joanne, are presenting Peg with a picture of the "Blue Madonna" by Carlo Dolci 1616-1687. The original Oil on canvas, 21" x 15 1/4" is in the John and Mable Ringling Museum of Art, Sarasota, Florida. Also is a copy of Bob's mom, Jane Kranich's poetry book, *Jesus Loves Us All*.

Curtis, Peg's son and Peg stand together in the newly painted main dinning room.

Curtis proudly stands next to his newly purchased pizza oven for making their New York style pizza.

9. A New Beginning

We are excited to announce that there is something new happening at Maria's Garden!

Curtis, Peg's son has taken over managing Maria's Garden. He is taking the burden off of Peg. Now she doesn't have to worry about managing and cooking. She can spend time with her patrons and be involved with her teaching moments.

Curtis is upgrading with new paint and décor. The main dining room has been painted with a light touch of blue and the icons are surrounded by blue violet which accents the gold frames. The tables now have deep blue black table cloths. The precious atmosphere of Jesus and Mary will remain.

Maria's outside Garden now has new umbrella covered tables and it even invites well-behaved pets to visit the garden with their masters.

Peg will be consulting so that all of her many delicious recipes and foods will continue to be available. A special edition is the newly purchased pizza oven to make New York style pizza.

Curtis plans to sponsor fund raisers for some local charities, such as the local SPCA as a starter. Maria's Garden will continue to be a witness for Jesus and Mary. Praise the Lord!

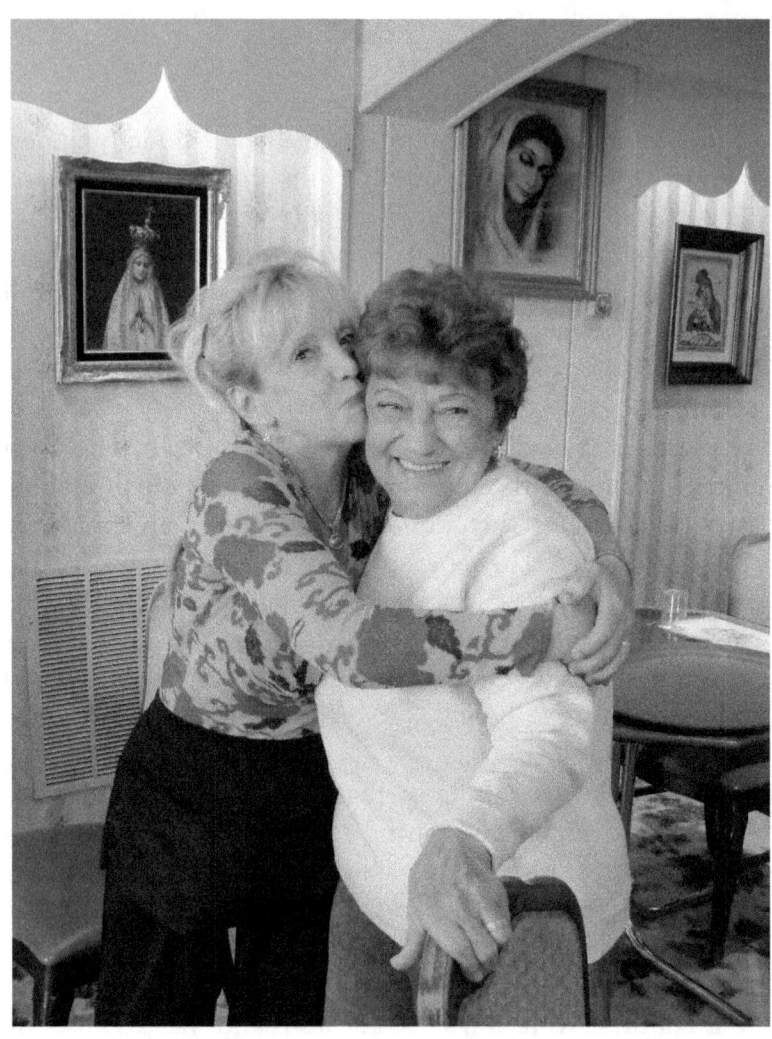
Peg and her daughter, Alesa. Alesa is a warm and vibrant lady.

10. In Conclusion

There is no doubt that Maria's Garden is a wonderful witness to *Mary, the Mother of God, and to God Himself.*

For we humans can not live forever, only the memories of what we have done. The basic test of an commercial establishment is to receive sufficient income to keep it operating, pay the workers, have excellence maintenance and go about its intended purpose.

Peg herself has unselfishly in slow times had to put in her savings to keep things going. "After all, my workers are a part of my Christian family, and all this is really my life's witness to Mary."

What about the "teachings"? How will this special witness continue after God calls Peg home?

We hope this book will help to preserve and encourage the ongoing of the deep and rich spiritual legacy of Maria's Garden.

Maria's Garden & Inn

There is a place in Berkeley Springs where time slows down...........................
There is a place where the weary traveler or tired worker may stop and rest......
There is a place where the home-cooked food will nourish and calm you..........
There is a place where the atmosphere is peaceful, comfortable and family........

Maria's Garden & Inn (Bed and Breakfast) is located three blocks from the center of the Berkeley Springs, West Virginia. It is nestled one block off the main street at the foot of the steep mountain that parallels the entire city. When you stay at Maria's you will want to park your car and not move it for your entire stay.

Leave the outside world and your troubles behind and enjoy the peaceful atmosphere. The wonderful home-cooked Italian food will nourish you and the serenity will calm you. You will go away refreshed and wanting to return.

The rooms of the Inn are entered through the doors of two identical very stately brick historic houses. The secret garden is nestled down in between the two houses and on the same lower floor as the dining rooms and kitchen. The entrance to the restaurant is on the lower floor. One may also enter the restaurant or rooms from the inside.

Maria's Garden & Inn (Bed and Breakfast) has an unbelievable collection of photos, statues, Icons and paintings These have been given to Maria's by friends and guests from throughout the country through the years. Even though there are religious artifacts on the walls and in the rooms of the inn, there is no feeling of intrusive religiosity.

Peg Perry was the owner, innkeeper and cook. She has trained her excellent staff with her Italian secrets from years of experience in the kitchen serving food to guests. You won't go hungry or broke. The food is wonderfully delicious, and the selection is plentiful. In fact you may decide to take all of your meals at the Inn.

In May 1, 2017 Peg signed over the management of Maria's Garden to her son, Curtis.

On a balcony overlooking the dining rooms the Inn has its very own chapel. It was built as a place of rest and solitude. It could be used for a small wedding.

Maria's Inn is decorated as an elegant B & B, with beautiful beds, spreads, furniture, accessories and bathrooms.

One side of the spacious porches.

Entering the Restaurant, one is greeted by beautiful Italian décor.

MARIA'S GARDEN & INN
42 Independence St.
Berkley Springs, W V 25411
304-258-2021

www.mariasgarden.com
info@mariasgarden.com

Isn't That Interesting!

bobkranich.com/books

www.ingramcontent.com/pod-product-compliance
Lightning Source LLC
Chambersburg PA
CBHW050603300426
44112CB00013B/2054